Phonics
Made Simple
·············

Grade 1

Written by Vicky Shiotsu
Illustrated by R. Michael Palan
and Becky Radtke

FS123307 Phonics Made Simple—Grade 1
All rights reserved–Printed in the U.S.A.
Copyright © 2000 Frank Schaffer Publications, Inc.
23740 Hawthorne Blvd.
Torrance, CA 90505

Editor: Jeanine Manfro
Art Director: Anthony Paular
Book Design: Rita Hudson
Graphic Artist: Randy Shinsato

Table
of Contents

ntroduction

Phonics is an important tool for understanding how written English "works." As children learn about the relationship between sounds and letters, they see that how a word is read or written is based on certain systematic rules.

any consonants nly make one ound.

The sounds of vowels vary.

Some onsonants can be grouped to form new sounds.

Learning phonics is an important key in learning how to read and write.

Reading and writing are essential skills of communication. An important part of acquiring these skills comes from a knowledge of phonetic rules and an understanding of how written English "works." *Phonics Made Simple—Grade 1* is designed to help teachers plan a phonics program that helps children become aware of the relationship between the letters of the alphabet and the sounds of English. The activities in this book incorporate a variety of experiences—visual aids, movement activities, poems, creative writing, and more—to make learning phonics both stimulating and rewarding. As students develop the ability to identify letters and to discriminate consonant and vowel sounds, they will be excited to learn that they can apply these skills in order to "figure out" what a word says or how to write words on their own. These early successes in reading and writing are crucial in the development of a child's self-confidence and self-esteem, and they lay the foundation for future learning.

....

Phonics Made Simple—Grade 1 can be used alone or as an integral part of any language arts program. The book is divided into four sections: *Consonants, Short Vowels, Long Vowels,* and *Consonant Blends and Digraphs.* Each section presents a variety of activities that are interesting, challenging, and grade-appropriate. The activities in each section may be introduced sequentially as they appear in the book or in random order.

3123307 Phonics Made Simple—Grade 1 ■ © Frank Schaffer Publications, Inc.

Consonants

Distinguishing the sounds of the consonants can be thought of as the "jumping-off" point from which young children begin learning how to read and write. Consonants produce sounds that are more consistent and more easily identifiable than vowels. When children learn to recognize the sounds of consonants (in both the beginning and final positions of words), they gain the ability to look at a word and make reasonable guesses as to what it might be. Helping children acquire a knowledge of consonants is essential to helping them understand how written English "works."

CONCEPTS

The ideas and activities presented in this section will help children develop the following skills:

- identifying beginning consonant sounds
- distinguishing between two or more beginning consonants
- identifying final consonant sounds
- distinguishing between two or more final consonants
- choosing words that have a particular beginning or final consonant

WHAT ORDER?

Organization

When teaching consonant sounds, you do not have to present the letters in alphabetical order. Many teachers, for example, introduce the sounds of *m* and *s* first because these letters appear most frequently in English. Whatever order you choose, make sure that you do not introduce two letters with similar sounds one after the other, such as *b* and *d*. Later, as children become more proficient in identifying consonants, similar sounds may be reviewed together to check for auditory discrimination.

PRESENTING A LESSON

Organization

Phonics lessons will vary regarding specific activities and content, but they should incorporate the following

1. <u>Auditory Stage</u>—In this stage, students listen for the sound they are learning. For example, you might state five words beginning with *b* and have the class name the common sound. Or, you could display objects that begin with *b* (such as a ball, book, and bell), and ask the children to name the items and state what the words have in common.

2. <u>Visual Stage</u>—In this stage, students see words containing a particular sound and identify the letter that produces the sound. For example, you might say three words ending with *m*, write them on the chalkboard, and ask the children to underline or circle the final letter of each word.

3. <u>Application Stage</u>—In this stage, students demonstrate that they understand the phonics concept. For example, they might brainstorm words that begin with *s*, make picture charts of objects that begin with *s*, or do reading and writing activities that reinforce the particular phonics concept.

Note: All three stages apply to any phonics lesson, and not just to lessons involving consonants.

FS123307 Phonics Made Simple—Grade 1 ■ © Frank Schaffer Publications, In

Beginning Consonants

CONSONANT BOOKLETS

Class Activity

Have the class make booklets that present the sounds of beginning consonants. First, give each child 6 sheets of drawing paper that have been folded in half. Staple the pages along the fold to make a booklet. Have each student write his or her name and the title *Consonants* on the first page. Students may also add colorful letters or other decorations. Tell the class that the remaining pages in their books will be used for the 21 consonant sounds.

Next, reproduce page 4 for every student, and have the children cut out the picture cards. Instruct the students to glue one card to the top of each page. Then when the students learn a consonant, have them find the corresponding page in the booklet. Have the class fill that page with pictures or words that represent the particular consonant sound. (Since very few words begin with *x*, have students think of words that *end* in that letter instead.)

CONSONANT COVER-UP

Class Activity

Use page 4 to check your students' knowledge of beginning consonant sounds. Hand out a copy of the page and several counters to each child. Then say a word, and have the students cover the consonant they hear at the beginning of the word. Repeat the activity several times, using a different consonant sound each time. You could adapt the activity to check students' discrimination of final consonant sounds. Instead of using page 4, prepare a similar grid that shows just the consonants. Then repeat the activity as described above, but have students cover the consonant they hear at the end of the word.

PICK A LETTER

Class Activity

Reproduce one copy of page 4 and cut apart the cards. Place the cards in a paper bag. Then call on one student at a time to draw a card from the bag, name the consonant, and state a word beginning with that letter sound. Let that child call on another student to draw a different letter. Repeat the activity several times.

Consonant Sounds

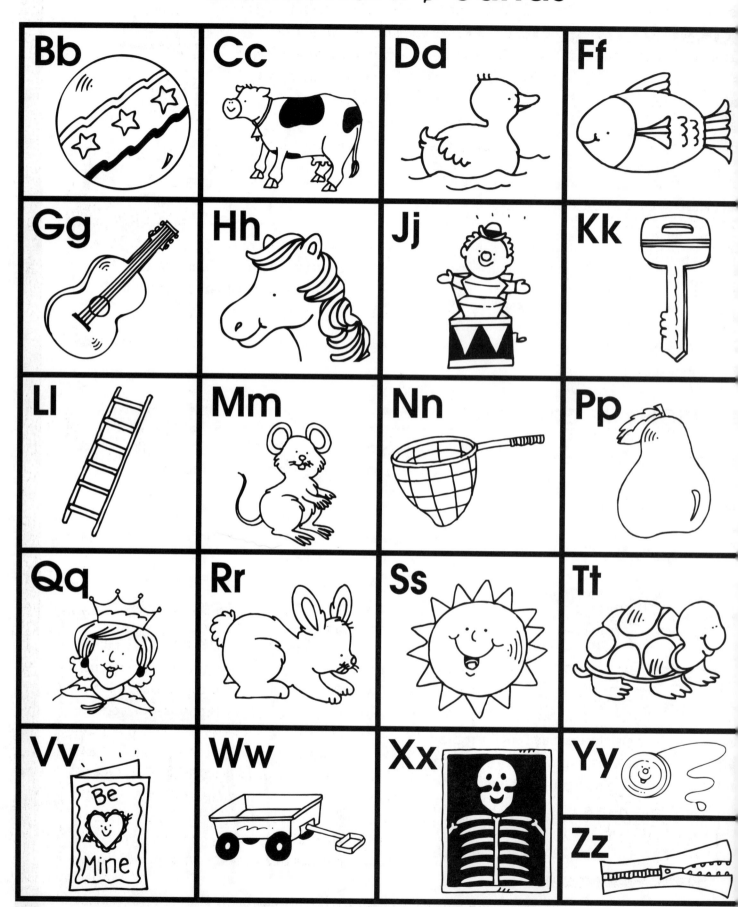

FS123307 Phonics Made Simple—Grade 1 ■ © Frank Schaffer Publications, Inc

THUMBS UP, THUMBS DOWN

Here's an easy activity that lets you check your students' auditory discrimination of consonant sounds. Students begin by sitting and forming fists with their hands. Tell the children that they will be listening for a specific consonant, such as *m*. Then say words, one at a time. Each time the students hear a word that begins with the designated consonant, have them hold their thumbs up. If they hear a word that begins with a different consonant, they place their thumbs down. Continue the activity for several minutes. As your class gains confidence in distinguishing consonants, increase the speed with which you say the words.

CONSONANT CATERPILLARS

Have the class make colorful caterpillars that display words beginning with a particular consonant. First, divide the class into small groups, and give each group several 4" circles cut from different colors of construction paper. Then tell the students that each group is to brainstorm words that begin with a particular consonant. Instruct the children to write or illustrate the words on the circles.

Next, have the groups tape or glue the circles together to form a caterpillar's body. Have the students add a circle that displays the consonant at the front of the body. Then have the children add a circle for the head; tell the children to glue on paper antennae and draw on facial features to complete their caterpillars. Afterwards, let the groups share their caterpillars and their words with the class.

Art Project

Consonant Collages

This fun activity reinforces the concept of beginning consonants. When teaching a consonant, brainstorm with the class a list of things that begin with that letter. Write the suggestions on the chalkboard. Next, give each child a sheet of heavy paper on which you've drawn the consonant as a large, block letter. Then have students fill in the letter by drawing or gluing on objects that begin with that consonant. For example, the letter *S* might be decorated with items such as sequins, gummed stars, seeds, and scraps of sandpaper. Display the completed letters on a bulletin board that has been titled *Consonant Collages*.

CONSONANT CARD GAMES

Use pages 7 and 8 to create games that help review the sounds of beginning consonants. (The consonant *x* is not represented in the set of pictures because there are so few words beginning with that letter.)

Memory Match

Divide the class into pairs, and reproduce pages 7 and 8 for each pair. Have the students cut out the cards on page 7 and glue them onto 2½" blue paper squares. Have them cut out the cards on page 8 and glue them onto 2½" red paper squares.

Next, tell the partners to lay their cards face down on a table or the floor. Instruct them to take turns picking up a red card and a blue card. If the two pictures begin with the same consonant, the child keeps the cards; if not, he or she returns them face down to their original positions. The game continues until all the cards have been picked up, and the partner with the greater number of cards wins.

Consonant Bingo

Give each student a sheet of paper with a grid showing sixteen 2" x 2" squares. Also give each student a copy of page 7 and 16 counters (beans, bingo chips, or other small items). Have the children cut out the pictures on page 7 and glue 16 of them onto their grids to make their bingo cards.

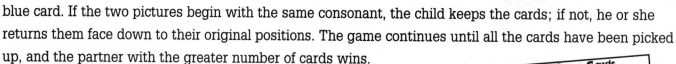

Reproduce one copy of page 8, and cut out the pictures to make calling cards. Place the cards in a paper bag. Then draw one card and call out the name of the picture. If students have a picture that begins with the same consonant, they place a counter over it. Continue drawing one card at a time and calling out the names. The first person to cover four pictures in a row wins the game and becomes the next caller.

Variation: Have each student write letters on their bingo cards instead of gluing on pictures. Then use either page 7 or 8 to make the calling cards. Play the game as described above.

Consonant Collection

Divide the class into four teams, and designate five consonants (excluding *x*) for each one. Reproduce one

copy of page 7 and one copy of page 8, and cut the cards apart. Place the cards in a paper bag. Call on one child to draw a picture card from the bag, name the picture, and state the beginning consonant. The team "collecting" that letter scores one point. Continue the procedure, calling on different students at a time to draw cards. The first team to score five points wins the game. (Teams do not have to score five points for five *different* letters. For example, a team collecting *b* scores two points if a picture of a bell and a picture of a bee are drawn.)

FS123307 Phonics Made Simple—Grade 1 ■ © Frank Schaffer Publications, Inc

Consonant Game Cards

Consonant Game Cards

FS123307 Phonics Made Simple—Grade 1 ■ © Frank Schaffer Publications, Inc

An Icy Path

Help the penguins get to the iceberg. Say the name of each picture on the path. Circle the beginning sound.

Name _____

 # Up, Up, and Away!

Look at the pictures behind each plane. Color the pictures that begin with the sound of the letter on the plane.

Hooray for Consonants!

Say the name of each picture. Write the letter that makes the beginning sound.

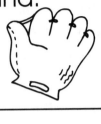

_____

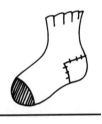

_____

_____

Final Consonants

LEARNING ENDING SOUNDS

As students become familiar with identifying beginning consonant sounds, they can also start distinguishin final consonant sounds. Here are some activities you can try.

▪ Say five words that end in the same consonant, such as *hen, pan, in, sun,* and *on.* Have the students state what the words have in common. Then write the words on the chalkboard and have the children identify the consonant that makes the sound.

▪ Say three words at a time, such as *pig, rug,* and *net,* and have the children identify the two words that end in the same consonant.

▪ Brainstorm a list of words that end in the same consonant. Then challenge the class to make sentences or poems using as many of the words as they can. Write their suggestions on a sheet of chart paper, and call on students to underline the appropriate words. Have the class read the sentences or poems together.

Ken can run
And play in the sun.
Ken can run
And have lots
of fun!

ERASE AWAY

Review final consonants with this quick activity. First, write six or seven consonants on the board. Then say a word that ends in one of the letters. Ask the class to identify the final consonant, and then call on a student to erase that letter from the chalkboard. Continue the activity until most of the letters have been erased.

BEGINNING, MIDDLE, END

Sharpen auditory skills by having students listen fo a consonant and identify its position in a word. For example, to reinforce the *t* sound, say these words one at a time: *tiny, hat, little, turtle,* and *tent.* As yo say each word, ask the class to state *beginning, middle,* or *end* to describe the *t*'s position.

Game

Trucking With Consonants

Reproduce the truck on page 14 for every student. Then have each student think of a word that begins and ends in a consonant, such as *bug*, and illustrate it in the middle of the truck. Have the student label the picture, and then write the beginning and ending letters to the left and right of it. Next, have the children fold along the dotted lines so that their pictures are covered. Let each child show his or her truck while the rest of the students look at the consonant clues and guess the picture inside. Afterwards, pin the trucks on a bulletin board to create a center where children can play the guessing game on their own.

Animals, Animals

Say the name of each animal. Circle the letter that makes the ending sound. Then color the pictures.

t z	g b	n l	v x
z g	b t	s b	g m
w n	l k	r d	p h

Trucking With Consonants

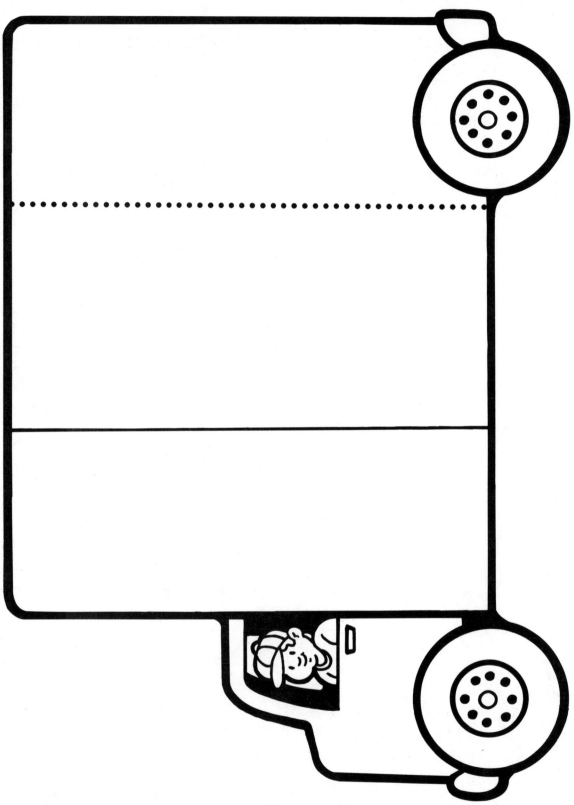

TEACHER: See page 12 for directions on using this page.

FS123307 Phonics Made Simple—Grade 1 ▪ © Frank Schaffer Publications, Inc

Beginning or End?

Say the name of each picture. If it **begins** with the circled letter, write it in the first box. If it **ends** with the circled letter, write it in the second box.

Going Home

Help the family get home. Write the missing letters for each word.

___ o ___ ___ e ___ ___ a ___ ___ i ___

___ u ___

___ o ___ ___ a ___ ___ i ___ ___ a ___

___ e ___

___ o ___ ___ e ___ ___ u ___

FS123307 Phonics Made Simple—Grade 1 ■ © Frank Schaffer Publications, Inc

Short Vowels

arning to hear, read, and write vowel sounds
n be a challenging task for children. Since
ritten English is not based on a purely phonetic
stem (the sound of long *a*, for example, can be
ritten as *ai, ay,* or *ei*), a child can still apply the
les of phonics and misread or misspell a word.
nce short vowels are more consistent in their
elling than long vowels, they are usually
troduced before the other vowel sounds. As
ildren develop an understanding of short
owels and are exposed to words that contain
asily identifiable letter/sound relationships, they
ain confidence in reading, spelling, and writing.

CONCEPTS

The ideas and activities presented in this section will help children develop the following skills:

- *identifying short vowel sounds*
- *distinguishing between two or more short vowels*
- *distinguishing rhyming words*
- *reading and writing short vowel words that have a consonant-vowel-consonant pattern*

ISTEN FOR THE VOWEL

Class Activity

When introducing a short vowel, use this activity to help you check
our students' auditory discrimination. Give each student an index
ard, and instruct the class to write *yes* on one side of the card and *no*
n the other. Then say a word, and have the students listen for the
hort vowel sound they are studying. If the word contains the vowel
ound, have the children hold up their cards with the *yes* side facing
ou. If the word does not contain the vowel, have them hold up the
ide that displays *no.* Continue the procedure with other words.

SHORT VOWEL CHARTS

Class Activity

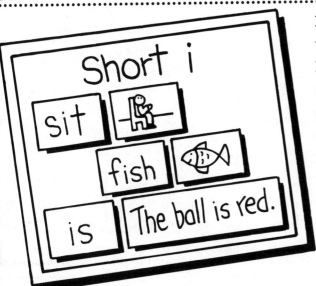

Have the students make a class chart that presents
words containing a specific short vowel sound. First,
have the class brainstorm words containing that vowel
sound, and write the words on the board. Next, have
each child write one of the words on a light-colored piece
of paper. Pass out additional papers so that children can
illustrate their words or write short sentences using
them. Finally, have the children glue their strips on a
sheet of chart paper to make a colorful display.

BOOKS

Books provide a concrete way for students to "see" how sounds are blended. To make a book, cut a 2" x 4" piece of tagboard. Then cut five or six 2" squares from lightweight paper. Attach the squares to the tagboard by stapling the pieces together along the short side. Next, write a short vowel word ending, such as *at* or *and* on the tagboard. On the squares, write consonants that can be added to the word ending to create a word. For example, the letters *b, c, h, r,* and *s* can be blended with *at.*

Make several sets of flip books to reinforce a short vowel sound. For example, to review short *a,* you might make sets for *-at, -and, -ast, -ag,* and *-ack* words. Let the children flip the cards and practice reading the words to one another. For a follow-up activity, have the students write sentences with some of the words.

SHORT VOWEL BOOKLETS

Have students make booklets each time you introduce a short vowel. Give each child a sheet of drawing paper and show the class how to fold the paper into fourths. Then have the students write words or sentences containing the short vowel they are learning in the sections created by the folds. Have children include illustrations in each section. Later, let the students read their booklets to the class.

Game

Rhyming Words Memory Match

Prepare 20 word cards that consist of 10 pairs of rhyming words that review a short vowel sound. For example, four cards for short *i* could be *pin, win, sit,* and *fit.* Then let small groups of children play with the cards. Instruct the students to lay the cards facedown on a table or the floor. Have the children take turns picking up two cards at a time. If the two words on the cards rhyme, the student keeps the cards; if not, the player returns them facedown to their original positions. The procedure continues until all the cards have been picked up. The player with the most cards wins.

Variation: Pair the children, and have partners make their own rhyming word cards. Then let the students play Memory Match with their partners.

SPOT THE VOWEL

several sentences to your students and have the class listen for words that contain the short vowel they studying. For example, if the class is reviewing short *i*, say sentences with two or more short *i* words: *s stick is thick. The pin is thin. Kim kicked the ball in the air.* As you say each sentence, have the dents identify the words containing the particular vowel sound.

Kim has six fish.

Next, write on the board other sentences that contain words with the short vowel your class is reviewing. Call on student volunteers to read the sentences and underline those words. Then let the children suggest other sentences, and write them on the board as well. Have the students spot the vowels and underline the appropriate words.

SENTENCE CHALLENGE

ainstorm with your class a list of words containing a particular ort vowel. Write the words on a sheet of chart paper. Then ide the class into pairs, and challenge each pair to write one or re sentences using as many of those words as possible. Later, the students to share their sentences with the class.

Fred will get a bell for his red sled.

Jen's hen has ten eggs in her nest.

WHICH VOWEL?

view short vowels with this easy activity. ve each child five paper squares, and tell the udents to write *a*, *e*, *i*, *o*, and *u* on them. struct the children to lay the letters in front of em. Then say a word with a short vowel und, such as *cup*, and have the students hold the vowel they hear. Continue the activity th other short vowel words.

terwards, students ore their ters in astic sealable gs for ture use.

Song

Action Fun

Sing this variation of "If You're Happy and You Know It," and review short vowels at the same time! First, discuss some actions that can accompany the song; tell the class that the action words must contain a short vowel. List the ideas on the board. Then sing the song, having the class do a different set of actions for each verse.

Here are some suggestions:

clap and snap (clap hands and snap fingers);

send a hello (say *Hello!*);

give a grin (smile);

jog on the spot (run in place);

rub your tummy (rub stomach with a circular motion).

Short A

LISTEN FOR SHORT "A"

Class Activity

Say the following words and have students point out the common sound: *apple, ask, act, ant, alligator*. Wr the words on the board, and have the children see that each word begins with *a*. Tell the class that the sound of the *a* in *apple* is called a short *a*. Next, have the children listen for the short *a* sound in these words: *bat, ran, dad, fan, bag*. Write the words on the board. Help the class see that the short *a* sound is i the middle of the word this time. Have the class name other short *a* words, and list their suggestions on th board. Then call on one student at a time to choose a word, read it aloud, and erase it.

ALLIGATOR, ALLIGATOR

Class Activity

Write the following chant on a sheet of chart paper:

Alligator, alligator,

What do you have?

I have an apple,

And, boy, am I glad!

Read the chant with your class. Then call on students to underline the words that have short *a*. Recite the chant again, this time clapping out the beat. Next, divide the class into small groups, and have each group write its own version of the chant by replacing *alligator* and *apple* with other short *a* words. Have the grou write their chants on sheets of paper and illustrate them. Later, let the groups read their chants to the clas

MYSTERY ITEMS

Class Activity

Fill a large shopping bag with several items that have short *a* in their names, such as a cap, mask, rag, can, and map. Then give clues to help your students guess what is in the bag. As each correct guess is made, take out that item and show it to the class. Invite your students to bring their own "mystery items" to place in the bag to review the short *a* sound. Let the children who bring the objects give the clues to the class.

Game

Apple Relay

Cut out ten or more paper apples, and write a short *a* word on each one. Make a second set of identical apples. Divide the class into two teams, and give each team a basket. Place the apples along a chalkboard ledge or on the floor several feet away from the teams. Then call out one of the words on the apples. The first person in each team runs and finds the corresponding apple, and places it in the basket. Continue the game until all the students have had a chance to run.

FS123307 Phonics Made Simple—Grade 1 ■ © Frank Schaffer Publications, I

Alley Cat's Sack

Inside Alley Cat's sack are things that have short **a** in their names. Look at the pictures below. Color the things that are in the sack.

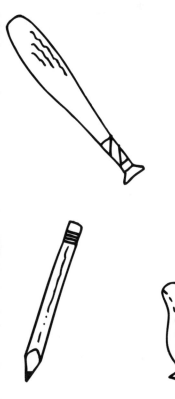

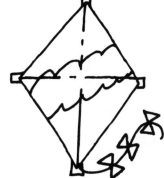

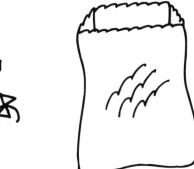

Read and **C**ircle

Read the words. Circle the word for each picture.

bag　bat	hat　had	fat　fan	cab　cat

pan　pad	rat　ram	mad　man	bag　bad

cast　cap	jam　jab	vat　van	tag　tack
	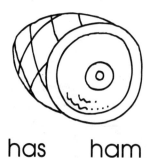		
sack　sad	has　ham	lad　lamp	hand　hat

Word Challenge

Cut out the letters. Put them together to make short **a** words. Write the words on the apple.

a **b** **c** **d** **m** **n** **r** **t**

Short I

LISTEN FOR SHORT "I"

Have students listen as you say these words: *it, is, in, ill, igloo.* Have the class notice that each word has th
same beginning sound. Write the words on the board, and have the children name the letter that begins
each word. Tell the class that the sound of the *i* in each of the words is called *short i.* Next, have the class
listen for the short *i* sound in these words: *pin, hill, sit, miss.* Write the words on the board. Help the class
see that the short *i* is in the middle of each word.

For follow-up, say several words one at a time as your class listens for the short *i* sound. If a word contains
short *i*, the students are to sit. If the word does not contain short *i*, the class is to stand.

SHORT "I" RIDDLES

Place the following items in a paper bag: a ribbon, an oven mitt, a ring, a safety pin, a dish, a bib, and a po
lid. Tell the class that you have several things whose names have a short *i* sound. Then give clues for each
item. Here are some suggestions:

> This can be used to tie your hair or wrap a present. (ribbon)
>
> This helps you take hot pans out of the oven. (mitt)
>
> This is something you wear on your finger. (ring)

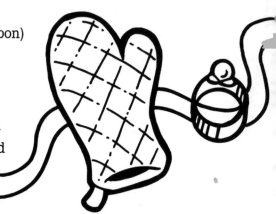

As each correct guess is made, take the item out of the bag and
write its name on the board. Afterwards, have the students read
the words together.

Game

Apple Relay

Cut out 12 or more fish shapes from colored paper. Tape a paper clip to one side of each fish.
On the other side, write a word that contains a short vowel. At least half of the words should
have short *i*. Make a fishing pole by tying string to one end of a
yardstick or dowel. Tie a magnet to the other end of the string.
Then lay the fish on the floor with the paper clips facing up.

Let three or four students at a time take turns "catching" fish
with the pole. When a student catches a fish, he or she looks at
the word and says it aloud. If the word contains short *i*, the
child keeps the fish. If not, he or she puts it back in its original
position on the floor. The first child to find four short *i* words
wins the game.

Time to Eat

Find pictures of words that have a short **i** sound. Color them red. Color the rest of the picture.

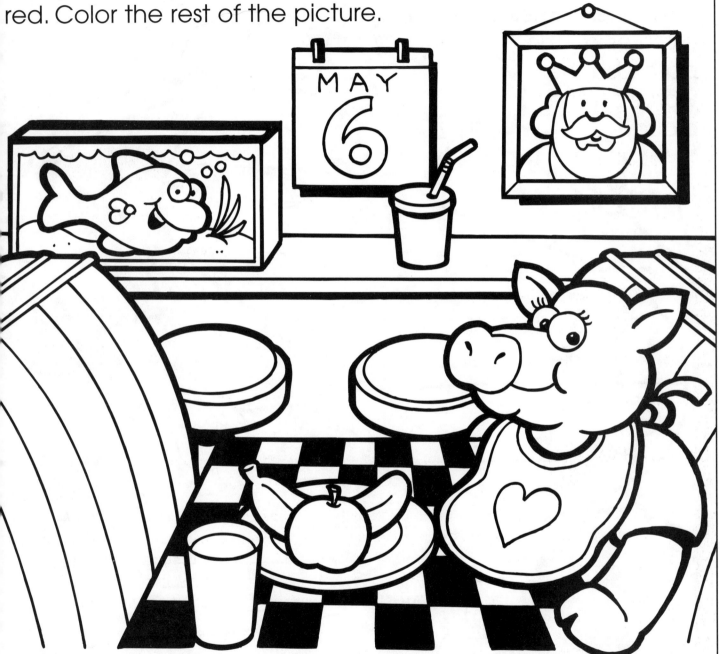

Circle the words that show the short **i** pictures you found.

king   fish   pin   bib   ring   dish   six   pig

Down the Hill

Help Jill get down the hill. Write the names of the pictures on the path. Use the words on the cloud.

pig   pin   fish   gift
wig   ring   mitt

reproducible

FS123307 Phonics Made Simple—Grade 1 ■ © Frank Schaffer Publications, In

Finish the **Sentences**

Write the correct word for each sentence.

1. Kim will sip the _____ .
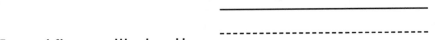
   mill   milk

2. Tim has a ball and a _____ .

   mitt   miss

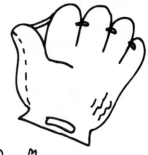

3. Here is a big _____ .
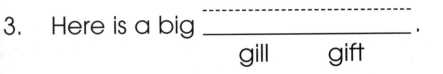
   gill   gift

4. I will _____ up the stick.

   pit   pick

5. The baby has a pink _____ .

   bib   big

6. The dish is in the _____ .
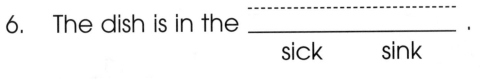
   sick   sink

Short O

LISTEN FOR SHORT "O"

Draw these objects on the board: box, sock, clock, toy block. Have the students name the pictures. Write the words below each one. Help students see that each word has a short *o* sound. Tell the class that the sound of the *o* in *box* is called short *o*.

Next, write the following words on the board: *rock, log, fox, doll, mop, pot, top, lock*. Then give clues and have the students guess the words. As each correct guess is made, call on a student to circle the corresponding word on the board.

A ROCKY PATH

Write short *o* words on paper rocks. Stand the rocks along a chalkboard ledge or pin them along the bottom of a bulletin board to make a path. Place a container of treats (such as stickers or jelly beans) at the end of the path. Then let each child try "hopping" down the path by reading the words aloud. As each child reaches the end of the path, reward him or her with a treat.

SHORT "O" SENTENCE CHALLENGE

Here's a fun way to help your students review short *o* words and create sentences with them. First, make flashcards of short *o* words. Place half the cards in a small box and the other half in a second small box.

Divide the class into two teams, and give each team a box of cards. Call on two students from one team to draw two cards from their box. Ask them to read the words aloud. The second team must then come up with a sentence using those two words. Once they decide on a sentence, write it on the board. Two students from the second team then draw two cards from their box and challenge the first team to make a sentence. Continue the activity until every student has had a chance to draw a card.

FS123307 Phonics Made Simple—Grade 1 ▪ © Frank Schaffer Publications,

What's Hiding?

Find out what is hiding below. If a space has a picture of a
short **o** word, color it red. Color the other spaces yellow.

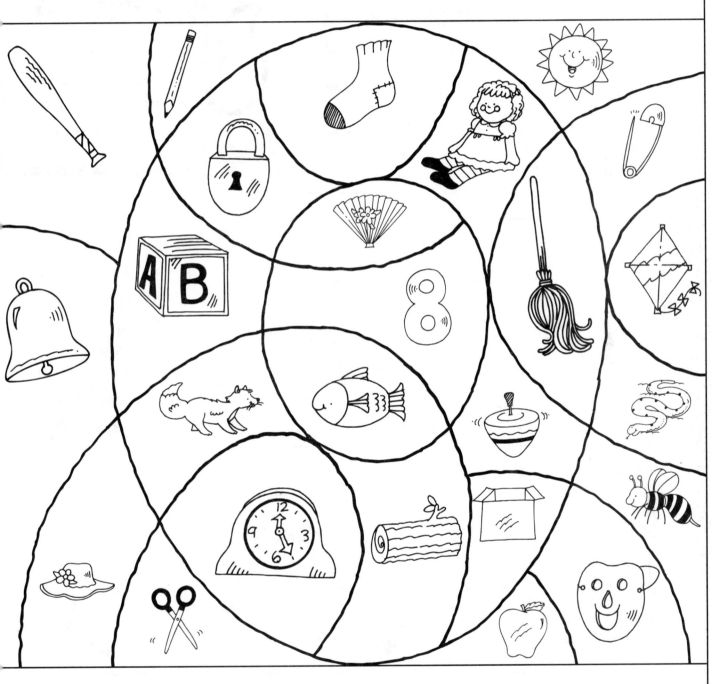

What was hiding? _____

Hunt for Short O

Dottie Fox looked in her home for things that have short **o** in their names. Read the list she made. Write each word under the matching picture.

pot	top
mop	doll
box	sock
lock	clock

_____
- - - - - - - - - - - -
_____

_____
- - - - - - - - - - - -
_____

_____
- - - - - - - - - - - -
_____

_____
- - - - - - - - - - - -
_____

_____
- - - - - - - - - - - -
_____

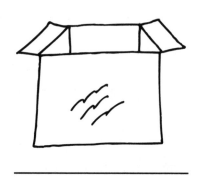

_____
- - - - - - - - - - - -
_____

_____
- - - - - - - - - - - -
_____

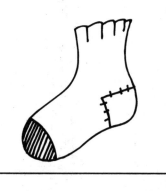

_____
- - - - - - - - - - - -
_____

FS123307 Phonics Made Simple—Grade 1 ▪ © Frank Schaffer Publications

Say the name of each picture. Color the ball **red** if its picture rhymes with . Color the ball **yellow** if its picture rhymes with .

Name _____

Cut and paste to match the pictures that have rhyming names

Nap has the **short** sound of **a**. Color each picture that has the **short a** sound.

Hat has the **short** sound of **a**. Cut and paste the pictures that have the **short a** sound.

Web has the **short** sound of **e**. Cut and paste the pictures that have the **short e** sound.

Name_____

Complete the crossword puzzle with words from the Answer List.

ANSWER LIST:

belt	nest	tent
desk	pencil	web
elbow	sled	wet
elephant	ten	yes

ACROSS

3. A large grey animal with a trunk is an _____.

5. You write with a _____.

8. You can slide down a snowy hill on a _____.

9. When you camp, you might sleep in a _____.

10. The opposite of **dry** is _____.

DOWN

1. In school, you might sit at a _____.

2. To hold your pants up, you can wear a _____.

3. Above your wrist is a joint called the _____.

4. Most birds lay eggs in a _____.

6. The opposite of **no** is _____.

7. A spider can spin a _____.

11. The number that comes after nine is _____.

62

Name _____

Sock has the **short** sound of **o**. Cut and paste the pictures that have the **short o** sound.

66

Name _____

Complete the crossword puzzle with words from the Answer List.

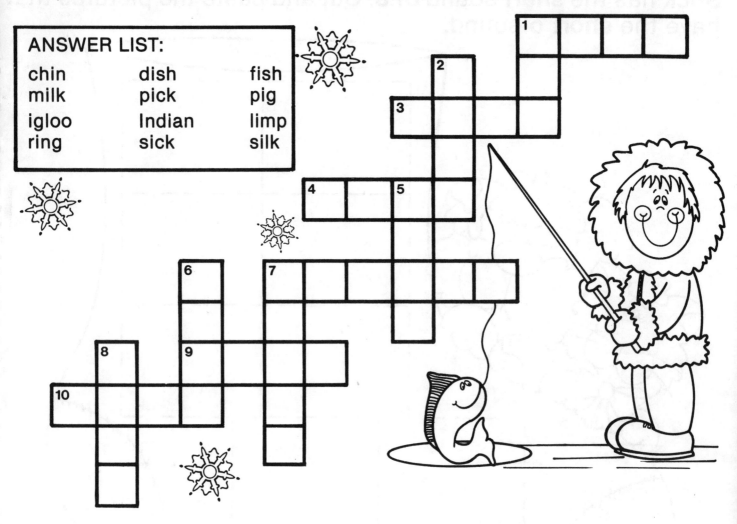

ANSWER LIST:

chin	dish	fish
milk	pick	pig
igloo	Indian	limp
ring	sick	silk

ACROSS

1. A word that means the same as **choose** is _____.
3. You wear this on your finger. _____
4. The opposite of **well** is _____.
7. This person sometimes wears a headband with feathers. _____
9. A soft, shiny fabric is _____.
10. With a rod and reel you can catch a _____.

DOWN

1. This farm animal oinks. _____
2. Babies drink a lot of _____
5. This part of your head is below your mouth. _____
6. Another name for a bowl is a _____.
7. Eskimos sometimes live in an _____.
8. If you sprain your ankle, you may walk with a _____.

ump has the **short** sound of **u**. Color each picture that has the
hort u sound.

Name _____

Truck has the **short** sound of **u**. Cut and paste the pictures that have the **short u** sound.

70

Which Sentence?

Copy the sentence that tells about each picture.

Tom sat on a log.
Tom sat on a dog.

_____

_____

A sock is in the box.
A doll is in the box.

_____

_____

Dot got a top.
Dot got a dog.

_____

_____

A fox is by a rock.
A fox is by a mop.

_____

_____

The pot is hot.
The pot is soft.

_____

_____

Short U

LISTEN FOR SHORT "U"

Ask the class which sound the following creatures have in common: bug, cub, duck, pup. Help the students see that each of the creatures has a short *u* sound in its name. Write the words on the board, and call on students to underline the *u*. Tell the class that the sound of the *u* in each of the words is called *short u*.

Next, list several short *u* words on the board, and have students read the words aloud. Include words in which the *u* is present at the beginning of the word, such as *up, us, under,* and *uncle.*

For a follow-up activity, check students' auditory discrimination of the short *u* sound by playing "Thumbs U Thumbs Down" as described on page 4.

ACTION FUN

Write these numbered sentences on strips of paper:

1. Jump up and down.
2. Run on the spot.
3. Rub your tummy.

4. Tap your desk like a drum.
5. Hum softly.
6. Walk like a duck.

Display the sentences. Have the class read the sentences aloud, and ask individual students to underline the short *u* words. Then call on students one at a time to roll a die and say the number that lands on top. Have the class read the corresponding numbered sentence and do the action that it describes. Repeat the activity until all the sentences have been selected at least once.

A BUG HUNT

Make flashcards of short *u* words. You will need at least as many cards as you have students. Draw a simple bug on the front (word side) of least half the cards. Then place the cards along the chalkboard ledge with their blank sides to the class.

Divide the class into two teams. Call on one student at a time from each team to pick a flashcard, read the word, and return to his or he seat with the card. When all the cards have bee picked, have the students count the number of bugs they collected. The team with the most bugs wins the game.

Plucky's Pictures

Plucky Duck drew pictures of things that have a short **u** sound. Look at the pictures below. Which ones did Plucky draw? Color them.

Rainy Day Puddles

Look at the pictures on the umbrellas. Write their names on the puddles. Use the words on the rain cloud.

cup   sun   jug   rug
bus   nut   bug   duck

_____

_____

_____

_____

_____

_____

_____

_____

Fun Day for a Cub

Cut out the sentences. Glue them under the matching pictures. Read your story.

1.

2.

3.

4.

| The cub sits in the mud. | The cub plays with a bug. |
| The cub runs up a hill. | The cub sits in a tub. |

Short E

LISTEN FOR SHORT "E"

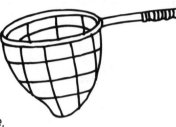

Make picture cards of a bell, the number 10, a nest, and a net. Label each picture. Show the cards to the class, and have the students read the words together. Help them see that each word contains a short *e* sound. Tell the class that the sound of the *e* in each of the words is called a short *e*.

Next, tape the cards along the top part of the chalkboard. Then write the following rhyming words under the corresponding pictures: under the bell, write *fell, sell, tell, well*; under the ten, write *den, hen, men, pen*; under the nest, write *best, rest, test, vest*; under the net, write *jet, met, pet, wet*. Show the students how to "blend" the sounds together to read the words. As the children say the words aloud, have them listen carefully to the sound of short *e*.

"EGG"CELLENT WORDS

tent

Write short *e* words on slips of paper, and place each slip inside a plastic egg. You will need enough eggs for four egg cartons. You may use a word more than once, but do not include the words in the same carton. Divide the class into four groups, and give each group a sheet of chart paper and one of the egg cartons. Instruct the students to open the eggs in their cartons and read the words. Challenge them to write sentences using as many of the short *e* words as they can. (Students may use more than one short *e* word in a sentence.) Have the groups write the sentences on their chart paper and underline the short *e* words they used. Afterwards, let the groups share their sentences with the class.

NAME RHYMES

Write the following sentences on the board:

Where is Ken? He's feeding the hen.

Where is Ted? He's sleeping in bed.

Where is Nell? She's ringing the bell.

Where is Bette? She's finding a net.

Have the students read the sentences and underline the short *e* words. Then brainstorm other sentences that can be added to the "name rhymes." Write the students' suggestions on the board. (Examples: *Where is Jen? She's lending her pen. Where is Fred? He's riding his sled.*) Read the sentences together. Have each student choose two or more of the sentences to write and illustrate on a sheet of paper.

Ed's Bedroom

Find pictures of things that have a short **e** sound in their names. Color them yellow. Color the rest of the picture.

Circle the words that show the short **e** pictures you found.

bell   bed   pen   desk   hen   nest   vest   net

Name _____

Get to the Tent

Help Nell get to her tent. Write the name of each picture on the path. Use the words on the log.

pen	web	tent
hen	jet	dress
bell	bed	sled

FS123307 Phonics Made Simple—Grade 1 ■ © Frank Schaffer Publications, Inc

Ted's Pet

Write the correct word on each line.

1. Ted jumped out of _____ .

   bed   best

2. He _____ to see his pet.

   west   went

3. His pet was a little _____ .

   hen   ten

4. The hen sat on a _____ .

   neck   nest

5. The nest had an _____ in it!

   egg   end

Draw an egg in the nest.

A Parade of Animals

Label the animals. Write **a**, **e**, **i**, **o**, or **u** on the lines.

c___t   d___g   p___g   f___x

h___n   b___t   f___sh   fr___g

b___g   r___t   y___k   d___ck

Name _____

Around the Home

Read the words. Circle the word for each picture.

bed bug	lamp limp	pot pet	sink sank
rug rig	fan fun	cup cap	desk dusk
lock lick	pin pan	met mat	tub tab
big bag	mop map	jog jug	pan pen

FS123307 Phonics Made Simple—Grade 1 ■ © Frank Schaffer Publications, Inc.

Long Vowels

Long vowels can be confusing for children because they are written in so many ways. For example, a child who writes *rane* for *rain* demonstrates an ability to apply phonics rules; the misspelling occurs because he or she has chosen a "wrong," though legitimate, way to note the long *a* sound. In addition, there are many exceptions to a spelling rule. *Cape, bike, have,* and *give* have a similar spelling pattern (long vowel with a silent *e*), but only *cape* and *bike* are pronounced with a long vowel sound. In spite of these discrepancies, phonics is still a useful tool for helping children learn to read and write. Continued exposure to written language helps children remember which words are spelled with which rules and which words are exceptions. The more children read and write, the more they learn about how English works, and the more they are able to deal with its inconsistencies.

LISTEN AND RUN — Class Activity

This outdoor activity will help you check your students' auditory discrimination of long vowels.

Take your students to a section of the playground where they can run. Tell the class that you will be saying several words. Whenever the students hear a word with the vowel sound they are learning (such as long *i*), they are to run to a designated place and back. Play this game until your class has run back and forth several times.

Variation: Divide the class into five groups and assign a long vowel to each group. Then call out a word with a long vowel. Students who have been assigned that vowel must run to the designated spot and back. Continue the activity until all students have had a chance to run.

CONCEPTS

The ideas and activities presented in this section will help children develop the following skills:

- identifying long vowel sounds
- distinguishing between two or more long vowels
- reading and writing long vowel words with silent *e*
- reading and writing words with vowel digraphs
- distinguishing between short vowels and long vowels

Word Collages

Group Activity

Divide the class into small groups, and have each group make a collage of words that have a particular long vowel sound. Have students look through magazines and newspapers, and let them cut out appropriate words. (If available, also have the students cut out accompanying pictures.) Tell the class that the words do not have to have the same spelling patterns. For example, if the students are studying long *a*, they may include words such as *cake, pail,* and *day.* Have group members glue their words on a sheet of butcher paper. Afterwards, let the students display their work in the classroom.

FS123307 Phonics Made Simple—Grade 1 ■ © Frank Schaffer Publications, Inc.

SILENT "E" BEE

Here's a visual way to reinforce the "consonant-long vowel-consonant-silent *e*" pattern. First, draw a bee on a piece of paper and write *e* in the middle of its body. Cut out the bee and tape it to a craft stick or ruler. Next, draw seven flowers on the board and write the following words on them: *cap, tap, fin, hid, hop, not, cub.*

Move the bee from flower to flower so that each time it is positioned at the end of the word. As you move the bee, have the class read the new words. For a follow-up activity, have students write sentences using these pairs of words: *can/cane, pin/pine, rob/robe, tub/tube.*

SPELLING PRACTICE FUN

Your students will enjoy practicing how to write long vowel words if you provide alternatives to paper and pencil. For example, let groups of students take turns writing on the board while you dictate words. Or, have students spell words by arranging magnetic letters on cookie sheets or tin lids. Some children may also be able to bring appropriate toys, such as small chalkboards or magnetic writing boards, to share with the class.

GIVE THE DOG A BONE

Cut out 20 or more bone shapes from white paper. Write short vowel words on half the bones and long vowel words on the other half. Place the bones in a paper lunch bag. Get two sheets of chart paper and draw a dog at the top of each one. Make one dog short and the other dog long. Post the chart papers at the front of the room.

Divide the class into two teams. Assign one team the short dog. Tell students on that team that they will be collecting short vowel words for their dog. Assign the other team the long dog, and tell those students they are going to collect long vowel words. Then have the teams take turns sending a student to draw a word from the bag. The student reads the word and tapes it to the appropriate chart paper. The first team to collect 10 bones wins the game.

Long A, Silent E

LISTEN FOR LONG "A"

Write the following words on the board and have your class read them aloud: *cap, tap, hat, can, pan*. Next, tell students that you will be changing each word. Then add an *e* to the end of each word and say the new words: *cape, tape, hate, cane, pane*. Ask students what sound they hear in all the words. Tell the class that the sound of the *a* in *cape* is called *long a*. Explain that whenever a vowel "says its name," it is called a *long vowel*. Help the class see that the *e* at the end of each word is silent but that it helps change the short *a* to long *a*.

For a follow-up activity, have students listen as you say several words with either a short *a* or long *a* sound, such as *cat, cake, hand*, and *late*. Instruct students to raise their right hands if a word has a short *a* and to raise their left hands if it has a long *a*.

A LONG "A" POEM

Write the following poem on a sheet of paper.

> Jake, Jake,
>
> What will you make?
>
> _____
>
> That's what I'll make.

Reproduce the poem for each student, and read the lines together. Next, brainstorm with students several phrases that can be inserted into the third line of the poem. Tell them that each phrase must contain one or more long *a* words. List the ideas on the board. (Examples: *a sweet birthday cake; a big wooden gate; a game about snakes.*) Then have each child write a phrase on his or her sheet of paper and illustrate the poem. Bind the pages together with front and back covers to make a booklet for the classroom library.

SLINKY SNAKES

Cut ovals from colored paper, and give several to each child. Then tell each student to draw a snake's face on one oval and write long *a* words with silent *e* on the other ovals. Have students tape their ovals together to form colorful snakes. Have students read their words to you before displaying the snakes around the room.

Name the Pictures

Label the pictures below. Use the words in the box.

cake	gate	tape
rake	vase	cane
cape	cave	game

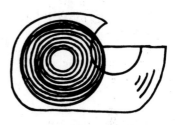

45

What Will They Do?

Look at the picture clues. Write the correct word for each sentence.

1. Dale will bake a _____.
   cake   cane

2. Jane will swim in the _____.
   late   lake

3. Nate will play a _____.
   game   gate

4. Dave will help Dad _____.
   rate   rake

5. Kate will wash the _____.
   plate   place

6. Jake will _____ at the rink.
   skate   snake

    FS123307 Phonics Made Simple—Grade 1 • © Frank Schaffer Publications, Inc

Long I, Silent E

LISTEN FOR LONG "I"

Write the following words on the board, one below the other: *pin, rip, fin, hid,* . Have the class read the words aloud. Then tell students that you can add something to *pin* to change the word into the name of a tree. Add *e* to the end *pin,* and have the class read the word with you. Next, ask a student volunteer add *e* to *rip* to change it to *ripe.* Continue the procedure with the other words. Tell students that the *i* sound in each of the words is called *long i.* Then *y* several words that have either the short *i* or long *i* sound. As you say each word, have students sit if the word has a short *i* and stand if it has a long *i*.

GO DOWN THE SLIDE

Draw a long slide on a sheet of butcher paper. Divide the slide into several sections, and write a long *i* word in each section. Then challenge students to go down the slide by reading the words from top to bottom. Afterwards, have students write sentences using as many of the words as they can.

bike
dime
like
nine
ride
tire
line
kite
time

LONG "I" RIDDLES

Write these and other riddles on slips of paper:

This is something you ride. (bike)

This is a long walk up a hill or mountain. (hike)

Bees live here. (hive)

This number is one more than eight. (nine)

This number is one less than six. (five)

A clock tells you about this. (time)

This is a color. (white)

Place the slips of paper in a paper bag. Then let students take turns drawing a riddle from the bag and reading it to the class. The child who guesses correctly writes the answer on the board and becomes the next person to select a riddle.

FS123307 Phonics Made Simple—Grade 1 ■ © Frank Schaffer Publications, Inc.

Find the Hive

Make a path to help the bee find its hive. Color the pictures that have long **i** in their names.

FS123307 Phonics Made Simple—Grade 1 ■ © Frank Schaffer Publications, Inc

Mike's Mice

Write the correct word for each sentence. Use the words from the box.

bike	hide	five
hike	nice	kite

1. Mike has _____ mice.

2. He rides with the mice on his _____.

3. Sometimes the mice _____ inside his pockets.

4. Sometimes they all go for a _____ up a hill.

5. The mice like to watch Mike fly his _____.

6. Mike thinks his mice are very _____!

Long O, Silent E

LISTEN FOR LONG "O"

Collect several of these items: a rope, a toy phone, a globe, an ice cream cone, a stone, and a chicken bone. Show the items one by one, and ask the students to name them. List the items on the board. Help the class see that all the words have a long o sound. Tell the class that the silent e at the end of each word "makes" the o say its name.

Next, write short o and long o words on the board, such as *hop, hope, rob, robe, not, note, hole, pot,* and *pole.* Have students take turns reading the words and circling the ones that have a long o sound.

LISTEN FOR THE PAIRS

Say three words at a time and have the class find the two words that have a long o sound. For example:

rob, rope, rose

home, bone, lot

stone, stop, stove

Continue the procedure with several groups of words.

A LONG "O" POEM

Write the following poem on the board:

I can dig a hole with a fishing pole,

I can, yes, I really can!

I can tell a joke while I'm wearing a robe,

I can, yes, I really can!

Have students read the poem together, and call on volunteers to underline the long o words. Then have students brainstorm other silly sentences containing long o words. (Examples: *I can talk a lot on the telephone; I can poke a hole in an ice cream cone; I can smell a rose with my sharp-smelling nose; I can spray my home with a garden hose.*) Write the suggestions on the board, and have the class recite the new versions of the poem. Later, have each child choose a line to illustrate, and display the drawings on a bulletin board.

Josie's Notes

Look at Josie's notebook. It shows some long **o** words. Write each word under its picture.

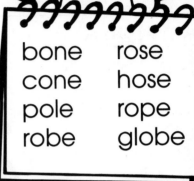

bone   rose
cone   hose
pole   rope
robe   globe

---

reproducible   **51**

Name _____

Let's Draw

Read the sentences. Underline the long **o** words.
Draw the pictures.

Draw a rose in the vase. 	Draw your home.
Draw a bone for the dog. 	Draw a long rope.
Draw a cone for the ice cream.	Draw a hole that the mole dug. 

FS123307 Phonics Made Simple—Grade 1 ▪ © Frank Schaffer Publications, In

Long U, Silent E

LISTEN FOR LONG "U"

Write the following words and have the class read them aloud: *cub, cut, tub*. Next, tell the class that you are going to change the words. Then add an *e* to the end of each word and have the students read the words with you. Tell the class that though the *e* is silent, it affects the way that the *u* sounds. Explain that when the *u* "says its name," the vowel is called long *u*.

For a follow-up activity, say several short *u* and long *u* words to the class, such as *jug, June, cup, cute, rug,* and *tune*. As you say each word, call on a student to write the word on the board and state whether the vowel is short or long.

INTERESTING WORDS

Since there are fewer long *u*/silent *e* words than there are long *a, i,* or *u* words, you may wish to introduce your students to new, interesting words that will give them added reading and writing practice with long *u*. Here are some words that may be appropriate for your class:

duke – a nobleman

dune – a mound of sand

mule – an animal that is born to a female horse

　　　　and a male donkey

mute – not able to speak

WORD DICE

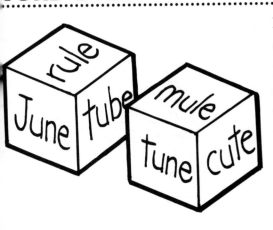

Make some "word dice" of long *u* words by writing the words on the sides of wooden blocks. Leave the dice along with pencils and sheets of writing paper at a center where children can work in small groups. Tell the students that when they work at the center, each of them gets one die. Each child throws his or her die, reads the word facing up, and writes a sentence with it. Tell the students to roll their dice at least four times; if the same word appears more than once, a child rolls until a different word is displayed.

Luke's Pictures

Look at the pictures that Luke drew. Circle their names. Write the words on the lines.

tub
tube

_____

sun
rule

_____

mud
mule

_____

cup
cute

_____

fun
flute

_____

bug
tune

_____

hut
huge

_____

duck
duke

_____

cub
cube

_____

FS123307 Phonics Made Simple—Grade 1 ■ © Frank Schaffer Publications, In

Read and Write

Write the correct word for each sentence.
Use the words in the box.

cute	tube
tune	mule
use	huge
cube	flute

_____

1. Let's hum a _____ .

2. May I _____ your glue?

3. An ice _____ is cold.

4. A _____ has four legs.

5. This pup is _____ .

6. This _____ is hard to open.

7. A whale is _____ .

8. Gus can play a _____ .

Run, Mice, Run!

Help the mice finish the race. Write **a**, **i**, **o**, or **u** on the lines.

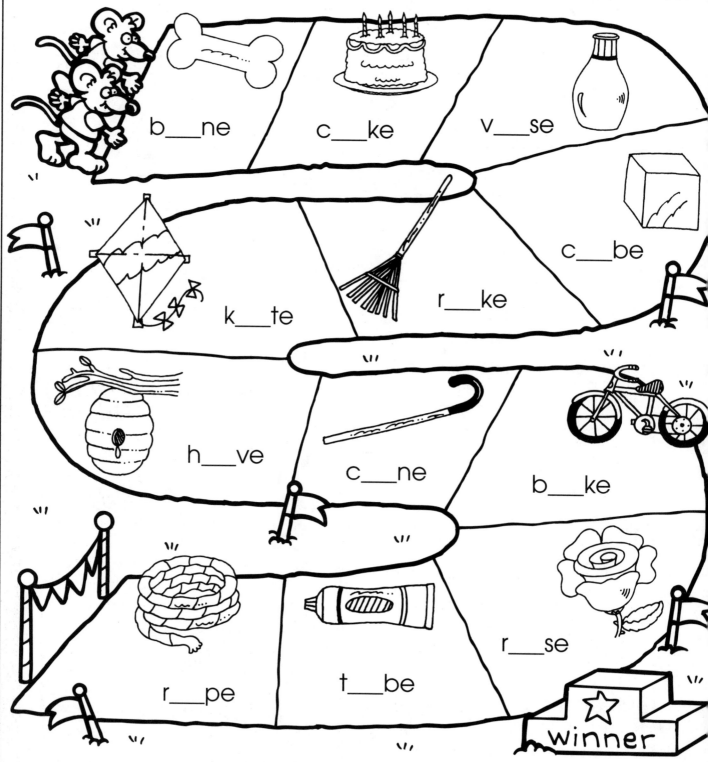

b___ne

c___ke

v___se

c___be

k___te

r___ke

h___ve

c___ne

b___ke

r___pe

t___be

r___se

winner

FS123307 *Phonics Made Simple*—Grade 1 ■ © Frank Schaffer Publications,

Vowel Digraphs

...raphs are two letters that produce a single sound, such as *ph* in *phone* or *ea* in *head*. In this section, ...'ll find activities for teaching the long vowel pairs *ai, ay, ee, ea* (as in *team*), and *oa*.

...TRODUCING VOWEL PAIRS — Class Activity ....

...sent vowel digraphs one at a time. For example, introduce *ai* words before presenting words containing ...When students are familiar with both pairs, let them work with *ai* and *ay* words together; afterwards, ...iew the various kinds of long *a* words they've learned so far (*ai, ay,* long *a* with silent *e*). Using this ...nulative approach, students gain phonics skills by building on what they already know.

...AIN, RAIN, GO AWAY — Group Activity ....

...re's a group activity that lets you reinforce students' ability to read words ...taining *ai* or *ay*. Cut out a large rain cloud from gray paper and pin it to a ...letin board. Cut out paper raindrops, and on each one write a word with *ai* ...ay. Pin the drops below the cloud. Next, call on several students to work ...h you at the bulletin board to help you make the rain "go away." Ask one ...ld to read a word on a raindrop, and then remove that drop from the ...letin board. Continue the procedure until all the drops have been removed.

...OATS AFLOAT — Class Activity ......

...t out paper boats and write an *oa* word on each one. ...st the boats on a bulletin board covered with blue ...per. Pin a piece of paper over each word to hide it. ...ite a number on each paper, and keep a numbered list ...owing which word is on which boat.

...ll students you need their help to keep the boats ...oat. Tell them they must guess the word on each boat ...d spell it correctly. Then give a riddle about one of the ...rds, such as *This is an animal with horns* (goat). The ...ild who guesses the word ...ells it aloud. If he or she ...sspells the word, another ...dent tries. If it is misspelled ...ain, the boat is taken away. ...ntinue the activity until all ...e words have been guessed.

Leafy Trees — Group Activity

Divide the class into small groups, and assign each group *ee* or *ea*. Then instruct each group to cut a tree trunk from brown paper and glue it onto a large sheet of paper. Have group members cut out paper leaves and write words containing their assigned vowel pair on each one. Let students look in dictionaries and library books for words they can use. Have students glue the leaves onto their trees for a colorful display.

Sailing Fun

Look at the picture on each sail.
Write its name on the line. Use
the words on the rock.

nail   pail
mail   tail
snail   rain
paint

FS123307 Phonics Made Simple—Grade 1 • © Frank Schaffer Publications,

What a Day!

Finish the sentences. Write the correct word on each line. Use the words in the box.

hay
play
clay
stay
gray

1. Kay went out to _____ / _____.

2. Faye's mule ate some _____ / _____.

3. Ray made a picture with a _____ / _____ crayon.

4. Jay made a vase from _____ / _____.

5. May had to _____ / _____ home and help her mom.

Draw a picture showing something you did today. Write a sentence about your picture.

Lee's Riddles

Write the answers to Lee's riddles.
Use the words in the box to help you.

| bee |
| eel |
| seed |
| feet |
| jeep |
| tree |
| sleep |
| teeth |

1. This has six legs. _____

2. This is a tall plant. _____

3. This helps you eat. _____

4. This is inside an apple. _____

5. You can ride in this. _____

6. This helps you walk. _____

7. You do this in your bed. _____

8. This lives in the water. _____

Dean's List

Help Dean finish his list of words. Write **ea** on the lines below. Then draw a line from each word to its picture.

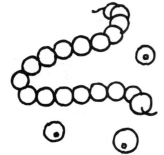

l___f

s___l

b___d

t___

b___k

m___t

b___n

p___s

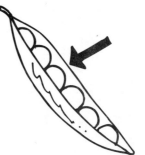

A Load of Words

Help the truck driver get the load to the store. Label the pictures on the road. Use the words in the cloud.

| goat | boat | coat | loaf |
| soap | coal | toad | toast |

A1·Market

Crossword Time

Read the clues. Fill in the puzzle.
Use words from the box.

Clues

Across
1. You can do this with a toy.
2. You ride this in the water.
4. Horses eat this.
5. You do this with food.

Down
1. You can use this to make a picture.
2. A bird eats with this.
3. This is a tall, leafy plant.

eat

beak

tree

hay

play

paint

boat

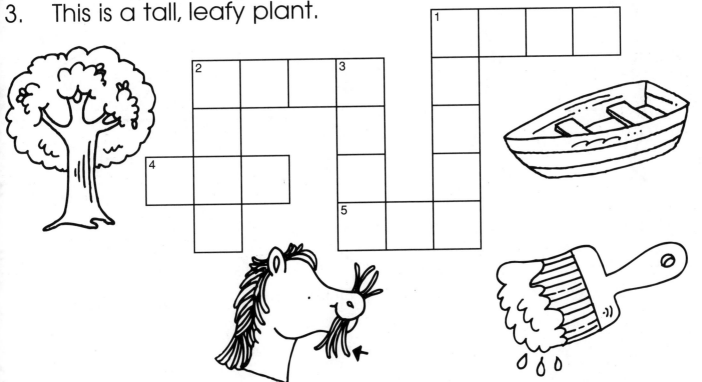

Name _____

Something to Ride

Read the words in the puzzle. If the word has a short vowel, color the space blue. If it has a long vowel, color the space yellow.

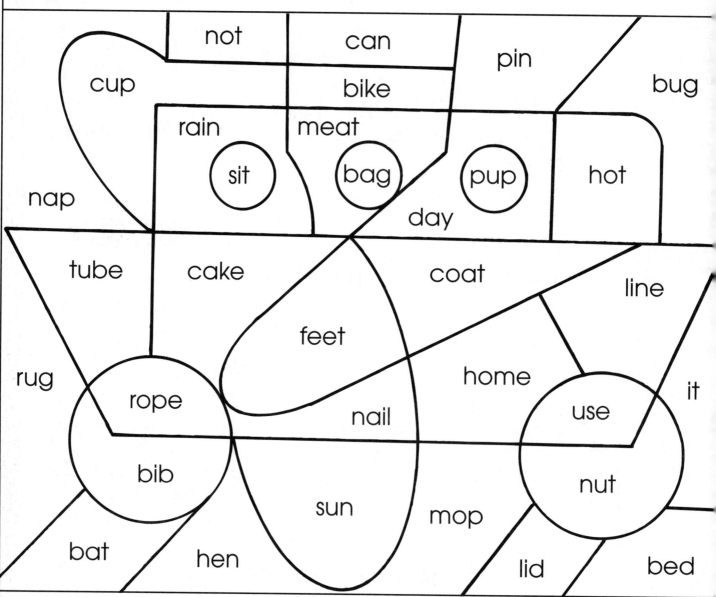

What did you find? Circle the answer.

jet   bus   boat   train   plane

Consonant Blends and Digraphs

nsonant blends are two or more consonants that combined to produce a "blended" sound, such the *bl* in *black* or the *st* in *stop*. Consonant raphs, on the other hand, are two consonants t form one sound, such as *ch* and *sh*. By the time ldren are working with blends and digraphs in eir phonics and spelling programs, they are eady familiar with short vowel and long vowel rd patterns. As they read and write words ntaining blends and digraphs, they will discover that if ey can read short and long vowel words such as *rag* and ke, they can apply similar phonetic rules to read words ch as *flag* and *shake*.

CONCEPTS

The ideas and activities presented in this section will help children develop the following skills:

- identifying consonant blends and digraphs
- distinguishing between two or more consonant blends
- distinguishing between two or more consonant digraphs
- reading and writing words with consonant blends and digraphs

Class Activity

Word Hunt

As you teach the individual blends and digraphs, challenge students to hunt for those letter combinations over several days. Have each child keep a running list of words found in newspapers, magazines, library books, food labels, TV commercials, and other materials. Tell students to also be on the lookout for certain letter combinations at the end of words, as in *roast, desk, bench,* and *dish*. Afterwards, have students make a class chart listing the words they found.

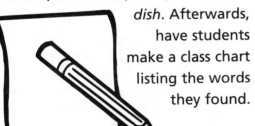

WORD WHEELS　　Visual Aid

Make word wheels that display words containing blends and digraphs. To make a word wheel, cut two identical circles from tagboard. Make the circles at least five inches in diameter. Cut out a "hole" about 1½" long and 1" wide from the edge of one circle. The hole should not be too close to the circle's center. Place the cut circle on top of the other, and attach the circles in the center with a brad fastener.

Write a consonant blend or digraph on the top circle, near the front of the hole. Write a word ending on the bottom circle so that the letters form a word. Turn the bottom circle so that you have space to write another word ending. Continue writing until you have at least five word endings on the bottom circle.

Store the word wheels in a box. Let students choose one, read the words, and write sentences with them. Or, have students work in pairs, choose two wheels, and take turns asking their partners to spell the words.

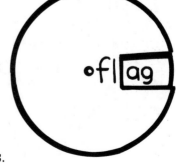

Consonant Blends

INTRODUCING BLENDS

Present consonant blends one at a time by saying words that contain the same blend and having students identify the common sound. For example, say *black, blue, blanket,* and *blink,* and have the class point out t *bl* sound; then write the words on the board, and call student volunteers to circle the blend in each word. Tell the class that consonant pairs such as *bl* are called blends because the two letters "work" together to form a combined sound.

There are three types of blends that first graders need to know—*l* blends, *r* blends, and *s* blends. Introduce each type separately before reviewing all three.

FUN WITH TONGUE TWISTERS

Write the following sentences on the board:

Blair blew blue bubbles.

Fran fried fresh fish.

Steve's starchy stew stuck on the stove.

Have the class read the sentences and ask individual students to underline the words containing blends. Tell the class that the sentences are called tongue twisters because they are hard to say. Then let students try saying the sentences aloud three times quickly. Afterwards, divide the class into small groups, and have each group make up tongue twisters containing blends. Have students write the sentences on sheets of paper and illustrate them. Bind the papers together to make a class booklet. Let the various groups challenge the class to say their tongue twisters.

BLEND BLOSSOMS

Brighten up your classroom with beautiful paper blossoms that displays blends. First, divide the class into pairs, and assign each pair a blend. Next, instruct the students to draw long, thin branches onto a 12" x 18" sheet of construction paper. Then have each pair cut out paper flowers and on each one write a word containing the particular blend. Have students glue the flowers onto the branches. Later, have the students read their words to the class.

What Will You Do?

Write the correct word for each sentence.
Use the words on the flags.

blocks

black   glass   clean   plant   flute

class

1. I will _____ my room.

2. I will play with some _____ .

3. I will get a _____ of milk.

4. I will _____ some seeds.

5. I will play a tune on my _____ .

6. I will get some _____ paint.

7. I will read a book to my _____ .

All Aboard!

Fill in the missing letters for each word. Use the letters on the train.

| br | cr | dr | fr | gr | pr | tr |

____og

____uck

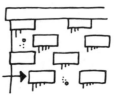
____ick

____apes

____um

____ize

____ab

____oom

____ee

____ess

____ass

____ib

Let It Snow!

Write the missing letters for the pictures on the snowballs.
Use the letters on the snowman to help you.

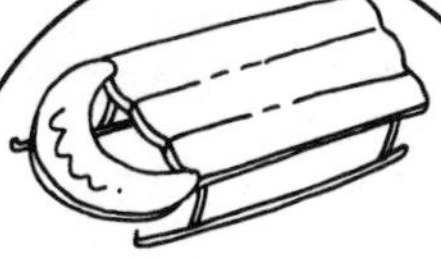

_____ed

_____ate

_____ick

_____ail

_____ide

_____ing

_____oke

_____unk

_____ar

_____oon

_____ake

_____amp

sk   sn
sl   sp
sm   st
sw

Look Carefully

Read the words. Circle the word for each picture.

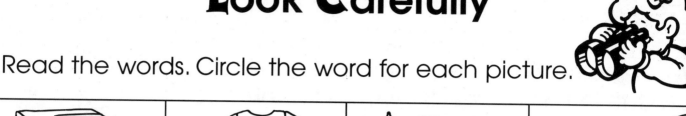

 block broke	 press dress	 flag float	 spoon stone
 glad plant	 smile slide	 smoke snake	 plane crane
 sling swing	 crock clock	 grass drape	 skate slate
 drain train	 snail smell	 grain glass	 spoke stove

FS123307 Phonics Made Simple—Grade 1 ▪ © Frank Schaffer Publications,

Consonant Digraphs

"CH" CHANT

Read the poem at the right with students, and have them make up actions for each line. Have them point out the words containing the *ch* sound. Then have the children brainstorm new lines for the poem, and write their suggestions on the board. Have the class say the new lines together. (Examples: *The engine on the tracks go choo, choo, choo! The children with their colds go ah-choo, ah-choo, ah-choo! The chalk on the board goes scritch, scritch, scratch. The bears eating berries go chomp, chomp, chomp!*)

The engine on the tracks goes chugga, chugga, chugga,

The logger with his ax goes choppa, choppa, choppa,

The mice with their cheese go pitter, pitter, patter,

And the chubby little chipmunk goes chitter, chitter, chatter.

LISTEN FOR "SH"

Ask students what sound people make when they want others to be quiet (*Shh!*). Have the class say the *sh* sound with you several times. Then say the following words one at a time, and have students state whether the *sh* sound is at the beginning or the end of the word: *ship, shoe, sheep, fish, wash, shop, wish, rush, hut.* For an extra challenge, call on students to spell the words after you say them.

MAKE "TH" WORDS

Write these words on the board: *thank, thick, think.* Help students see that the words begin with the same sound. Circle the *th* in each word, and have students practice saying *th-th-th* by placing their tongues between their teeth and blowing gently without making a sound. Then say the following words to students, and have them say the corresponding *th* words that rhyme: *pin/thin; ring/thing; sigh/thigh; bird/third; corn/thorn; crumb/thumb.* (Words such as *the* and *there* have the voiced *th* sound, and should be kept separate in your introductory lessons of *th*.)

A WHEEL OF WORDS

Use this game to reinforce the reading of *wh* words. Draw a large wheel on a sheet of butcher paper. Between the spokes, write words beginning with *wh*. Post the wheel on a wall. Next, blindfold a student and have the child stand a few feet away from the wheel. Have the child walk to the wheel and place a self-sticking removable note on it. Then undo the blindfold and ask the child to read the word closest to the note and to use the word in a sentence. Continue the game with other students.

FS123307 Phonics Made Simple—Grade 1 ■ © Frank Schaffer Publications, Inc.

A Chain of Words

Write the correct word for each sentence.
Use the words inside the chain.

chop   chess   chick   chair   check   chest   cheese

1. A _____ is a baby chicken.

2. I will eat some _____ for lunch.

3. Sandy plays _____ at school.

4. Dad will _____ some wood.

5. You may sit in this _____ .

6. Please _____ to see if the meat is cooked.

7. Jan keeps her rings inside a little _____ .

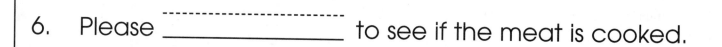

Shayne's Homework

Help Shayne with her work. Write the word for each picture below. Use the words in the box. Circle the **sh** in each word you write.

ship	shelf	fish
shade	sheep	dish
shell	sheet	brush

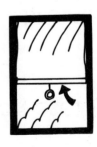

Name _____

Think Hard!

Write the correct word for each sentence.

1. Brad will _____ Theo for helping him.
   think   thank

2. This paper is _____.
   thin   thing

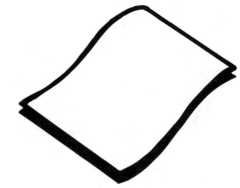

3. Thelma is the _____ girl in the line.
   thirst   third

4. What is that big _____ in the box?
   think   thing

5. This _____ coat will keep me warm.
   three   thick

6. A rose has sharp _____.
   thorns   thumps

FS123307 Phonics Made Simple—Grade 1 • © Frank Schaffer Publications, In

A Whale of a List

Read the words on the whale. Use them to write the missing word for each sentence.

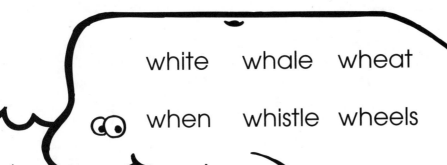

white   whale   wheat

when   whistle   wheels

1. A _____ lives in the sea.

2. A wagon has four _____.

3. Farmer Jones grows _____.

4. Eggs can be brown or _____.

5. I will blow my _____.

6. The cat ran _____ she saw the dog.

What Sound?

Say the name of each picture. Circle the letters that make the beginning sound.

	ch sh th wh		ch sh th wh		ch sh th wh		ch sh th wh
	ch sh th wh		ch sh th wh		ch sh th wh		ch sh th wh
	ch sh th wh		ch sh th wh		ch sh th wh		ch sh th wh
	ch sh th wh		ch sh th wh		ch sh th wh		ch sh th wh

FS123307 Phonics Made Simple—Grade 1 ■ © Frank Schaffer Publications, I

ge 8
ese letters should be circled for
following pictures: fork–*f;* leaf–*l;*
–*k;* sun–*s;* vase–*v;* pie–*p;*
k–*b;* table–*t;* cake–*c;* mask–*m*

ge 9
ese letters should be circled for
following pictures: balloon–*b;*
–*t;* yo-yo–*y;* doll–*d;* fan–*f;* jacks–*j;*
–*k;* paintbrush–*p;* car–*c;*
nkey–*m;* wagon–*w;* net–*n*

ge 10
ese pictures should be colored:
ck and door; house and heart;
der and lock; pear and pillow;
w and sail.

ge 11

ge 13
ese letters should be circled for
following pictures:
–*t;* dog–*g;* hen–*n;* fox–*x;* pig–*g;*
at–*t;* crab–*b;* frog–*g;* lion–*n;*
al–*l;* bird–*d;* sheep–*p*

ge 15

ge 16
ese words should be completed
the path: mop, net, fan, six, rug,
g, pin, hat, log, web, top, bed,
n.

ge 21
ese pictures should be colored:
t, cap, apple, mask, fan, stamp,
g.

Page 22
These words should be circled:
bat, hat, fan, cat
pan, rat, man, bag
cap, jam, van, tack
sack, ham, lamp, hand

Page 23
Words will vary.

Page 25

These words should be circled: king,
fish, bib, dish, six, pig.

Page 26
These words should be written on
the path: pin, pig, ring, wig, mitt,
fish, gift.

Page 27
1. milk   2. mitt
3. gift   4. pick
5. bib   6. sink

Page 29

What was hiding? O

Page 30
top, pot
clock, lock, mop
box, doll, sock

Page 31
Tom sat on a log.
A doll is in the box.
Dot got a dog.
A fox is by a rock.
The pot is hot.

Page 33
These pictures should be colored:
cup, bug, bus, sun, drum, truck.

Page 34

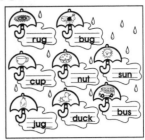

Page 35
1. The cub plays with a bug.
2. The cub runs up a hill.
3. The cub sits in the mud.
4. The cub sits in a tub.

Page 37

These words should be circled: bed,
pen, desk, nest, vest, net.

Page 38
These words should be written in
this order on the path: pen, bed,
bell, hen, jet, sled, web, dress, tent.

Page 39
1. bed
2. went
3. hen
4. nest
5. egg
An egg should be drawn in the nest.

Page 40
The names of these animals should
be completed: cat, dog, pig, fox,
hen, bat, fish, frog, bug, rat, yak,
duck.

Page 41
bed, lamp, pot, sink
rug, fan, cup, desk
lock, pin, mat, tub
bag, mop, jug, pen

Page 45
rake, cave, tape
gate, vase, game
cake, cape, cane

Page 46
1. cake
2. lake
3. game
4. rake
5. plate
6. skate

Page 48

Page 49
1. five   2. bike
3. hide   4. hike
5. kite   6. nice

Page 51
rope, pole
cone, rose, globe
robe, hose, bone

Page 52
Pictures should be drawn according to the directions.

Page 54
tube, sun, mule
cup, flute, bug
hut, duck, cube

Page 55
1. tune   2. use
3. cube   4. mule
5. cute   6. tube
7. huge   8. flute

Page 56
bone, cake, vase, cube, rake, kite, hive, cane, bike, rose, tube, rope

Page 58

Page 59
1. play
2. hay
3. gray
4. clay
5. stay
Picture and sentence will vary.

Page 60
1. bee   2. tree
3. teeth   4. seed
5. jeep   6. feet
7. sleep   8. eel

Page 61
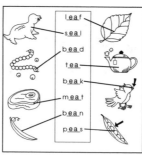

Page 62
The words should be written on the path in this order: soap, coal, toad, loaf, goat, coat, toast, boat.

Page 63
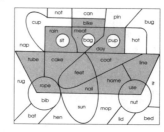

Page 64
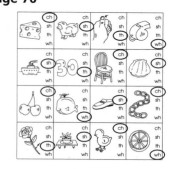

boat

Page 67
1. clean   2. blocks
3. glass   4. plant
5. flute   6. black
7. class

Page 68
frog, truck, brick, grapes
drum, prize, crab, broom
tree, dress, grass, crib

Page 69
These words should be completed
sled, skate, stick, snail, swing, slid
smoke, skunk, star, spoon, snake,
stamp.

Page 70
block, dress, flag, spoon
plant, slide, snake, plane
swing, clock, grass, skate
train, snail, glass, stove

Page 72
1. chick   2. cheese
3. chess   4. chop
5. chair   6. check
7. chest

Page 73
shell, sheep, dish
shelf, fish, ship
sheet, brush, shade
The *sh* in each word should be circled.

Page 74
1. thank   2. thin
3. third   4. thing
5. thick   6. thorns

Page 75
1. whale   2. wheels
3. wheat   4. white
5. whistle   6. when

Page 76